MAVIS BEACON

Teaches Typing™

A Brief Course

Lawrence W. Erickson, Ed.D.
Professor of Education, Emeritus
University of California
Los Angeles, CA

D0154691

Indian Prairie Public Library District
401 Plainfield Road ~ Darien, IL 60561

THOMSON
★
SOUTH-WESTERN

Australia · Canada · Mexico · Singapore · Spain · United Kingdom · United States

THOMSON™

SOUTH-WESTERN

Mavis Beacon Teaches Typing™
A Brief Course
By Lawrence W. Erickson Ed.D.

Vice President/Editorial Director:
Jack Calhoun

Vice President/Editor-in-Chief:
Dave Shaut

Senior Publisher:
Karen Schmohe

Acquisitions Editor:
Jane Congdon

Consulting Editor:
Dianne Rankin

Production Editor:
Carol Spencer

Production Manager:
Patricia Boies

Executive Marketing Manager:
Carol Volz

Marketing Manager:
Mike Cloran

Marketing Coordinator:
Cira Brown

Design Project Manager:
Stacy Jenkins Shirley

Internal Design:
Joe Pagliaro Design

Cover Design:
TLC Properties, LLC.

Compositor:
Cover to Cover Publishing, Inc.

Printer:
Quebecor World, Dubuque

Rights and Permissions Manager:
Linda Ellis

Senior Print Buyer:
Charlene Taylor

For more information, contact
South-Western
5191 Natorp Boulevard
Mason, OH, 45040.

Or, visit our Internet site at
www.swlearning.com

For permission to use material from this text, contact us by
Tel: (800) 730-2214
Fax: (800) 730-2215
Web: www.thomsonrights.com

CONTENTS

Lesson 1
Home Keys (fdsa jkl;)

Objectives

1. To improve control of home keys (**fdsa jkl;**)
2. To improve control of **Space Bar** and **Return/Enter** keys.

1A Work Area Arrangement

Arrange your work area as shown below.

- alphanumeric (main) keyboard directly in front of chair
- front edge of keyboard even with edge of table or desk
- monitor placed for easy view
- disk drives placed for easy access and disks within easy reach (unless using a network)
- book at right of keyboard

Properly arranged work area

31C Focus @, #, &, and ^ Keys

1. Locate the @ (at), # (number/pound), & (ampersand), and ^ (caret) keys on the keyboard chart at the right. Practice the reach to each key.

2. Key the lines twice; SS with a DS between 2-line groups.

Practice Guide

Reach to each new key with the correct finger:

@ (at)—left third finger and **Right Shift**

(number/pound)—left second finger and **Right Shift**

& (ampersand)—right first finger and **Left Shift**

^ (caret)—right first finger and **Left Shift**

1 s@s s@s @ s @ s @ $2; @ $5; smith@aol.com; @s@ s@s
2 d#d d#d #d# # # 45# 67# #90 #89 93# 10# #26 d#d d#

3 j&j j&j &j& &j& & & May & June; March & April; j&j
4 j^j j^j ^j^ ^j^ ^ ^ ^s ^to ^no ^t ^23 ^now ^ed ^es

5 JNeal@kih.com; BThomas@kal.us; two @ $5; one @ $41
6 Buy 12# of #10 nails and 6# of #8 nails for a job.

7 He will visit Brown & Yung, CA&O, and Mark & Beck.
8 The ^ mark may be used to mark insertions in text.

31D Build Skill

Key the lines twice; SS with a DS between 2-line groups.

Spacing Guide

- Do not space between # (number/ pound) and the number that comes before or after it.

- Space before and after & (ampersand) when used between words.

1 Cindy's shoes cost $12 (+ tax) on sale at 50% off.
2 "The file [letter_9] was sent to mavis@power.net."

3 "*Note" marked the reference for a home-town team.
4 Checks #129, #140, and #141 were not in the stack!

5 Perry & Charles is a builder; LU/J is a decorator.
6 The number < 102 was 81; the number > 142 was 147.

7 Use the ^ symbol to mark words inserted on a page.
8 We use the = (equal sign) in formulas: 4 + 4 = 8.

1B Keying Position

Follow these guidelines for proper position.

Position Guide

- fingers curved and upright over home keys
- wrists low, but not touching keyboard
- forearms parallel to slant of keyboard
- body erect, sitting back in chair
- feet on floor for balance
- eyes on copy

Proper keying position

1C Focus on Home Keys

1. Place your hands in home-key position (left-hand fingers on **f d s a** and right-hand fingers on **j k l ;**).
2. Key the lines once; single-spaced (SS) with a double space (DS) between 2-line groups. Do not key line numbers.

Practice Guide

Strike each key with a light tap with the tip of the finger, snapping the fingertip toward the palm of the hand.

```
1   ff jj ff jj fj fj dd kk dd kk dk dk ff jj dd kk fj
2   ss ll ss ll sl sl aa ;; aa ;; a; a; ss ll aa ;; sl

3   a; sl dk fj a; sl dk fj asdf jkl; asdf jkl; a;sldk
4   asdf jkl; asdf jkl; a; sl dk fj a; sl dk fj a;sldk

5   asdf jkl; asdf jkl; a; sl dk fj a; sl dk fj a;sldk
6   ff jj fj fj dd kk dk dk ss ll sl sl aa ;; a; a; fj

7   dad dad sad sad lad lad lass lass fad fad jas jass
8   dal dal kad kas lak lak lad; sad; fad; kal; dad; ;;
```

Lesson 31
@, #, &, and ^ Keys

Objectives

1. To improve control of @ (at), # (number/pound), & (ampersand), and ^ (caret) keys.
2. To improve control of **Space Bar**, **Tab**, and **Return/Enter** keys.

31A Review

Key the drill lines twice. SS lines and DS between 2-line groups.

All Letters 1 Jack Z. Vaughn quickly fixed the main power boats.

All Numbers 2 Jean bought clothes for $12.98, $4.50, and $36.75.

Space Bar 3 My men may help Jim draw a map of the swampy farm.

Speed 4 The city chairman may pay the men for their visit.

31B Improve Techniques

1. Use the default tabs for your word processor or set tabs at 1' intervals.
2. Key the lines twice; SS with a DS between 2-line groups. Strike the **Tab** key where a → (right arrow) appears.

Tab Control

1 $438 → 72% → y-axis → Bob's → "Now!"

2 1/2 → 3/5 → 7/9 → 4/7 → 2 1/2

3 (How?) → (Who?) → [Why?] → [yes] → [no]

4 3 + 2 → 4 < 8 → 10 > 2 → = 20 → = 30%

5 *Note I'm; 2 + 2 = 4; (See page 24.) 3/4; *Source

Space Bar 6 (no) (yes) [2 pages] [1 doz.] "Yes!" 4% + 2% = 6%

7 The cat and rat ran up and down the wet gray walk.

8 Mercury Mars; Earth Venus Saturn; Jupiter Neptune;

Shift Key 9 The Nortons, Browmans, and Jacksons left the fair.

10 Sue NcNulty and Ellen James live in Waverly, Iowa.

Lesson 2
H and G Keys

Objectives

1. To improve control of **h** and **g** keys.
2. To improve control of **Space Bar** and **Return/Enter** keys.

2A Review

Key the drill lines at the right. SS lines and DS between 2-line groups.

Practice Guide

- Keep your eyes on the book.
- Key at a steady, even pace.
- Strike each key with a quick-snap stroke.

```
1   asdf jkl; asdf jkl; a; sl dk fj a; sl dk fj a;sldk
2   asdf jkl; asdf jkl; a; sl dk fj a; sl dk fj a;sldk

3   a d kk jj a a ;; ss da sa kd la sl las add lad dad
4   jj ff kk dd ll ss ;; aa asdf jkl; fdsa ;lkj sad; ;

5   as lad lad; ask ask; add add dad dad sad; sad lass;
6   fall; fall; add; ask; ask; dad; dad; sad; add; dad;
```

2B Focus on H and G Keys

1. Locate the **h** and **g** keys on the keyboard chart at the right. Practice the reach to each key.
2. Key the lines twice; single-spaced (SS) with a double space (DS) between 2-line groups.

Practice Guide

Reach to each new key with the correct finger:

    g—left first finger

    h—right first finger

```
1   jh jh hj hj hh ha ha had had has h hh half half ha
2   fg gf gg fg gf gas gas sag sag gag gag gas sag sag

3   hh hh hh ha ha had had has had hag hag had has gag
4   gas gas had has had had sag sag glass; glass flash

5   gall gall gas gas; had had; half half sag; sag gas
6   half half had had gag gas glass glass sag sag flash
```

30C Focus on *, =, <, and > Keys

1. Locate the * (asterisk), = (equal), < (less than), and > (greater than) keys on the keyboard chart at the right. Practice the reach to each key.

2. Key the lines twice; SS with a DS between 2-line groups.

Practice Guide

Reach to each new key with the correct finger:

* (asterisk)—right second finger and **Left Shift**

= (equal)—right fourth finger

< (less than)—right second finger and **Left Shift**

> (greater than)—right third finger and **Left Shift**

```
1   k*k k*k *k** *Note *Example *k* *Note *Sample *See

2   ;=; ;=; =;= = = 2 + 2 = 4; 4 + 4 = 8; 3 + 3 = 6; =

3   k<k k<k k<k <k< 2 <4; 5 < 7; 3 < 16; < 75%; < 100;
4   1>1 1>1 >1> >1> 4 > 2; 12 > 3; > 20; > $45; > 200;

5   Yes, 90% of the students scored > 75%; some > 90%.
6   The problem that Karl solved was 5x > 10 but < 20.

7   He used the * to mark a source note in that paper.
8   "*Note", "*Source," and "*See" are usual examples.
```

30D Check Progress

1. Set the line spacing to DS, and set a 0.5" tab. Key the paragraph at a slow, controlled pace.

2. Key one or more 1' timed writings on the paragraph. Determine your rate. Try to increase your speed on each timing.

```
              •              4          •            8
     The < and > keys are used in keying formulas.
     •            12         •           16         •
The = and + are also used for this purpose.  The *
  20          •            24          •            28
key is used to mark a reference note.  I can
     •            32        •           36
strike all the keys with a light touch.
```

2C Build Skill

Key the drill lines at the right. SS lines and DS between 2-line groups.

Spacing Guide

- Do not space between a ; (semicolon) and the word it follows.
- Space once after a ; (semicolon).

```
1  g gf hag hag had has ask hag ask dad gf gas gas gf
2  g gf hag hag had has ask hag ask dad gf gas gas gf

3  h hh a aa ha ha d dd dad dad had had ha had dad ha
4  h hh a aa ha ha d dd dad dad had had ha had dad ha

5  ask half; ask dad; sad dad; glass; ash; gall hall;
6  ask half; ask dad; sad dad; glass; ash; gall hall;

7  flash; gas; gall, half, hall, salsa; gad gaff; gad
8  flash; gas; gall, half, hall, salsa; gad gaff; gad
```

2D Improve Techniques

Key the drill lines at the right. SS lines and DS between 2-line groups.

Practice Guide

- To improve keystroking, align fingers correctly.
- Strike each key with a quick-snap stroke.

Correct finger alignment

```
1  g gf hag hag had has ask hag ask dad gf gas gas gf
2  g gf hag hag had has ask hag ask dad gf gas gas gf

3  half a glass, a sad lass had a fall; ask all lads;
4  half a glass, a sad lass had a fall; ask all lads;

5  asdf jkl; a;sldkfj had ask lag flag sag; ask a lad
6  asdf jkl; a;sldkfj had ask lag flag sag; ask a lad

7  as dash glad gag lad fad dad ask a lad; half flash
8  as dash glad gag lad fad dad ask a lad; half flash
```

Lesson 30
*, =, <, and > Keys

Objectives

1. To improve control of * (asterisk), =(equal), < (less than), and > (greater than) keys.
2. To improve control of **Space Bar**, **Tab**, and **Return**/**Enter** keys.

30A Review

Key the drill lines twice. SS lines and DS between 2-line groups.

All Letters 1 Quincy jumped over freezing water with lock boxes.

All Numbers 2 I bought 20 rods for $4.89 and 3 reels for $16.75.

Finger Action 3 After you were here, I asked him to serve for you.

Speed 4 I gave my name and asked for the date of the case.

30B Improve Techniques

1. Use the default tabs for your word processor or set tabs at 1' intervals.
2. Key the lines twice; SS with a DS between 2-line groups. Strike the **Tab** key where a → (right arrow) appears.

Tab Control

1 $629 → 46% → to-do → May's → "Go!"
2 3/4 → 2/3 → 7/8 → 4/5 → 1/2

3 [1] → [2] → [3] → [4] → [5]
4 1 + 2 → 3 + 4 → 9 + 5 → 2 + 0 → 6 + 8

5 81% $29 I'll [no] [yes] 4 + 4 $53.89 "How?" [n/a]

Space Bar 6 can't don't won't does you're we're we'll I'm I'll

7 Memo_2 is the file name Sue will use for the memo.

8 Monday Tuesday Wednesday Thursday Friday Saturday;

Shift Key 9 Flo, Minnie, Tiger, Fluff, and Bobbie are my cats.

10 Flynn was born on April 2; Paul was born on May 1.

Lesson 3
I, T, and M Keys

Objectives

1. To improve control of **i**, **t**, and **m** keys.
2. To improve control of **Space Bar** and **Return/Enter** keys.

3A Review

Key the drill lines at the right. SS lines and DS between 2-line groups.

1 h h hj a aa d dd had had s ss has has k kk ask ask
2 g gf hag hag had has ask hag ask dad gf gas gas gf

3 flag; flag; fall fall lass; dash; sash; flash gall
4 lad; dad; sad; has; had; gag; ha; half; half glass

3B Focus on I, T, and M Keys

1. Locate the **i**, **t**, and **m** keys on the keyboard chart at the right. Practice the reach to each key.
2. Key the lines twice; SS with a DS between 2-line groups.

Practice Guide

Reach to each new key with the correct finger:

    i—right second finger
    t—left first finger
    m—right first finger

1 i i ik ik if if if; t t tf tf fit fit fit; if it k
2 m m mj mj jam jam jam; if fit jam; if it is a fig;

3 i i ik ik t t tf tf; m m mj mh; if it is; if it is
4 if it is fig jam; mail it; mail it; till till; tam

5 am am tam tam; mill mill lima lima kit kit fat fat
6 mall mask miss mist mist; stall tall talk tag tad;

29C Focus on +, /, [, and] Keys

1. Locate the + (plus), / (slash), [(left bracket), and] (right bracket) keys on the keyboard chart at the right. Practice the reach to each key.

2. Key the lines twice; SS with a DS between 2-line groups.

Practice Guide

Reach to each new key with the correct finger:

+ (plus)—right fourth finger and **Left Shift**

/ (slash)—right fourth finger

[(left bracket)—right fourth finger

] (right bracket)—right fourth finger

Spacing Guide

■ Do not space between a figure and the / (slash).

■ Do not space between a [(left bracket) or a] (right bracket) and the copy enclosed.

1 ;+; ;+; 2 + 2 ;+; 3 + 4 9 + 8 4 + 9 5 + 0 45 + 231

2 ;/; ;/; /;/ /;/ 3/4 1/2 5/6 7/8 in/out and/or ;/;/

3 ;[; ;[; ;[; ;]; ;]; [] [] [No] [Yes] ;[; ;]; [] []

4 ;+; ;+; 43 + 56 89 + 23 45 - 3 + 2 3 + 3 + 5 8 + 2

5 Key 2 3/4 and 7/8 and 9/10 and 4/5 and 2/3 and 56.

6 "He was quoted in a magazine article [May, 2003]."

7 "The problem [20 + 2 3/4] was very easy to solve."

8 The owner/manager [Zackra Parsons] saved 10% + 5%.

29D Check Progress

1. Set the line spacing to DS, and set a 0.5" tab. Key the paragraph at a slow, controlled pace.

2. Key one or more 1' timed writings on the paragraph. Determine your rate. Try to increase your speed on each timing.

```
                    •           4              •            8
       Today I learned the [ and ] keys.  Now I can
     •             12            •           16          •
key $ and ' and % and " and ( and ) and _ and !,
    20              •           24          •           28
or I can key 5/6 and 50+ and -32.  I key well with
    •              32
my fingers curved.
```

3C Practice the Left Shift Key

Key the drill lines twice. SS lines and DS between 2-line groups.

Technique Guide

To key the capital letters of keys controlled by your right hand, use the left shift key.

1. Locate the **Left Shift** key on your keyboard.
2. Place your fingers on the home keys. Reach with your left fourth (little) finger to the **Left Shift** key.
3. Press the **Left Shift** key all the way down while you strike the a letter key with a finger on your right hand.
4. Release the **Left Shift** key and quickly bring your finger back to home position.

Left Shift reach

1 Ja Jam Ka Ka La La Jam Lam; Mall Jim Lass It Is If
2 If it is fig jam; I shall mail it; I shall mail it

3 Mail it; Jim had half a glass; Jim had a flag; Kal
4 Jim had fig jam; Lil has a fig; Kal is at; It is I

5 Hall Half If I Kas Lil Mill Mall Lima Mist Miss If
6 Lima had it; Lil is; Miss Jama; Mad Jim; If I; Kas

3D Improve Techniques

Key the drill lines twice. SS lines and DS between 2-line groups.

Practice Guide

- Speed up your Space Bar action. Use a quick down-and-in motion of the thumb.
- Key steadily without pauses.
- Be ready to strike each key by reading ahead of the key are you striking.

1 am jam did if till mill mall lad sad flash half at
2 add hall dad did ham if jam fig mail it is I am at

3 It is a gag; a lad has; Lima is at; It is; Hal has
4 Lil has a mill; dad had; flash; Gill is; glass had

5 I had a dad; Lila is at a mall; ask Jima if it is;
6 Jill had a flag; Kill; Kill; film; film; aim; Half

Lesson 29
+, /, [, and] Keys

Objectives

1. To improve control of + (plus), / (slash), [(left bracket), and] (right bracket) keys.

2. To improve control of **Space Bar**, **Tab**, and **Return/Enter** keys.

29A Review

Key the drill lines twice. SS lines and DS between 2-line groups.

All Letters 1 Brave puzzled ibex fought with many quiet jackals.

All Numbers 2 Buy 149 books, 30 pencils, 265 pens, and 78 boxes.

3rd & 4th Fingers 3 Paula saw a plump squaw as she colored wax apples.

Speed 4 He may go with them when they go to sign the form.

29B Improve Techniques

1. Use the default tabs for your word processor or set tabs at 1' intervals.

2. Key the lines twice; SS with a DS between 2-line groups. Strike the **Tab** key where a → (right arrow) appears.

1 $209 → 64% → U-turn → can't → "Good!"

2 $837 → 205% → X-ray → Joe's → "Stop!"

Tab Control

3 (1) → (2) → (3) → (4) → (5)

4 1. ___ → 2. ___ → 3. ___ → 4. ___ → 5. ___

5 70% $129 I'm tune-up 23% 43% $29 $98.33 "Go!" 52%

Space Bar 6 them am not can do may was had did up see now your

7 Sam_memo T-shirt f-stop x-axis A-frame "Now!" most

8 March April May June July August October December;

Shift Key 9 Tomas and Kim met Quinn and Jonathan after school.

10 On June 1, Andy left Crete and moved to Minnesota.

Lesson 4
E, O, and X Keys

Objectives

1. To improve control of **e**, **o**, and **x** keys.
2. To improve control of **Space Bar** and **Return/Enter** keys.

4A Review

Key the drill lines twice. SS lines and DS between 2-line groups.

Practice Guide

Key without looking at the keyboard.

```
1   Has had; is all; fall flag Jim lags asks dad sail;
2   Jim had fig jam; ask did it it is a gag; a lad has

3   till mall; mitt jam tam tag Lima; sit had fit kill
4   as sad dad fall gas half jam kilt; flag glass ham;
```

4B Focus on E, O, and X Keys

1. Locate the **e**, **o**, and **x** keys on the keyboard chart at the right. Practice the reach to each key.
2. Key the lines twice; SS with a DS between 2-line groups.

Practice Guide

Reach to each new key with the correct finger:

    e—left second finger

    o—right third finger

    x—left third finger

```
1   e e ed ed ded he he o o ol ol doe do x x sx sx six
2   ed he; do ol; He has six doe; she did fix the mix;

3   e ed he; o ol doe; x xs six; the six doe; ed ol xs
4   do six sex flex sole old sold fax lax fold told of

5   Joe asked to see the fox; six dogs ate the old jam
6   tax six fox mold taxi flex logs mix heed lead deed
```

28C Focus on (,), _, and ! Keys

1. Locate the **(** (left parenthesis), **)** (right parenthesis), **_** (underline), and **!** (exclamation) keys on the keyboard chart at the right. Practice the reach to each key.

2. Key the lines twice; SS with a DS between 2-line groups.

Practice Guide

Reach to each new key with the correct finger:

((left parenthesis)—right third finger and **Left Shift**

) (right parenthesis)—right fourth finger and **Left Shift**

_ (underline)—right fourth finger and **Left Shift**

! (exclamation)—left fourth finger and **Right Shift**

Spacing Guide

- Do not space between parentheses and the words within them.
- Space twice after an **!** (exclamation) at the end of a sentence.

> **Rule**
>
> Strike the **_** (underline) several times to create a blank.

1 1(1 1(1 ((;); ;); ;); ;_; ;_; ;_; (Age) (Date) _

2 1(1 1(1 ;); ;); ((See page 10.)   (See example A).

3 ! a!a a!a !a! Go!   Stop!   Wait!   No!   I will!   No!

4 Leave now!   The game was great!   Josh was excited!

5 Name: _____ Date: _____ Age: _____

6 Hint: (1) depress shift; (2) strike key; (3) key.

7 Steps: (1) clear tabs; (2) set tab; (3) key text.

8 Ready!   Set!   Go!   Run faster!   Jump higher!   Now!

9 Miranda Jones (the new sales manager) read a list.

10 Your office is open late on Monday (until 9 p.m.).

11 The food was good!   Zeb scored 100%!   Go home now!

12 The file name I used last was Report_Wilson_1.doc.

13 Class: _____ Room: _____ Grade: _____

14 I finished the difficult job (and it wasn't easy)!

4C Build Skill

Key the drill lines twice. SS lines and DS between 2-line groups.

Practice Guide

- Keep fingers curved when reaching to the third and first rows.
- As you strike each key, try to fix that key location in your mind.

```
1   a;sldkfj a;sldkfj ff jj dd kk ss ll aa ;; a;sldkfj
2   had had; has has; ask ask; hag hag; lad lad; flag;

3   Jim Jim; if fit; jam jam; he he; doe doe; six six;
4   ff jj fj fj; dd kk dk dk; ss ll sl sl; aa ;; a; a;

5   h hj hj had; a aa ah; d dd dad; s ss has; k kk ask
6   g gf gf hag; l ll lad; f ff flag; j jj jig; ; ;; ;

7   i ik ik if; t tf tf fit; m mj mj jam; e ed ed the;
8   o ol ol doe; x xs xs six; the dog if jam six flask
```

4D Improve Techniques

Key the drill lines twice. SS lines and DS between 2-line groups.

Check Techniques

- Fingers curved and upright?
- Hands and arms quiet?
- Down-and-in spacing motion?

```
1   asdf jkl; a; sl dk fj a;sldkfj a;sldkfj a;sldkfjgh
2   gf gf jh jh; ik ik tf tf; mj mj ed ed; ol ol xs xs

3   head heed lead keel eel egg safe feed foe feel sea
4   old sold mold told hold home roam roll oil soil of

5   tax lax six; sex mat time till atoll atom; tome at
6   flex; flax; foam; exit; exist; taxi; exam; loam ox

7   I like fig jam; half a mill; He has six dogs I do;
8   Joe asked to see the fox; six dogs ate the fig jam
```

Lesson 28
(,) , _ , and ! Keys

Objectives
1. To improve control of **(** (left parenthesis), **)** (right parenthesis), **_** (under-line), and **!** (exclamation) keys.
2. To improve control of **Space Bar**, **Tab**, and **Return/Enter** keys.

28A Review

Key the drill lines at the right. SS lines and DS between 2-line groups.

All Letters 1 Wave amazed Jack by escaping quickly from the box.

All Numbers 2 Robert will add 10 3/4, 56 1/2, and 19 7/8 for me.

Double Letters 3 Bill will soon feel better about free book offers.

Speed 4 Both men may sign the forms for the big city firm.

28B Improve Techniques

1. Use the default tabs for your word processor or set tabs at 1' intervals.
2. Key the lines twice; SS with a DS between 2-line groups. Strike the **Tab** key where a → (right arrow) appears.

Tab Control
1 $145 → 83% → go-to → don't → "Yes."
2 $120 → 150% → say-so → we'll → "No."

Space Bar
3 and the and the and the and the and the and the an
4 Many busy men in my firm may meet in the key city.

Shift Key
5 Jan, Sue, and Hal may go to St. Paul or St. Louis.
6 Jack Flynn, Al Dulles, and Paul McNeil saw Robert.

One-Hand Words
7 You are the only tester who can state union facts.
8 Are you aware that those weavers were ill at home?

Lesson 5
N, R, and . Keys

Objectives

1. To improve control of **n**, **r**, and . (period) keys.
2. To improve control of **Space Bar** and **Return/Enter** keys.

5A Review

Key the drill lines twice. SS lines and DS between 2-line groups.

Practice Guide

Keep your wrists low and relaxed.

1   e ed he; o ol doe; x xs six; the six doe; ed ol xs
2   Jim had a dog; ask to see the fox; a lad got lost;

3   Hal likes jam; the six dogs; all of the kids lost;
4   Make it go; Kim is here; Joe has a glass; I do see

5B Focus on N, R, and . Keys

1. Locate the **n**, **r**, and . (period) keys on the keyboard chart at the right. Practice the reach to each key.
2. Key the lines twice; SS with a DS between 2-line groups.

Practice Guide

Reach to each new key with the correct finger:

   n—right first finger

   r—left first finger

   . (period)—left third finger

1   n n nj nj an an; r r rf rf for for; . . .l .1 La.;
2   I shall do it. Jan or I shall do it all for them.

3   n nj an; r rf for ; . .1 .1; an and; or for; nj rf;
4   His name is Dan Lee. Ask Jim or Sam or Al for it.

5   Nan or I shall fix the fig jam and send it to Kim.
6   Manfred is alert. Ronda learned to steer. I ran.

27C Build Skill

Key the lines twice; SS with a DS between 2-line groups.

Spacing Guide

- Do not space before or after a - (hyphen).
- Do not space between a " (quotation mark) and the material you are quoting.
- Do not space between a % (percent symbol) and the number that comes before it. Space once after the %.

Rule

Type the - (hyphen) twice to make a -- (dash). Do not space before or after a dash.

1 He did a bang-up job on the play-off schedule map.

2 "Malam's home isn't on the left-hand side, is it?"

3 "Jan's score is 95%." "Lu-Ann needs $12 for now."

4 Carla-Rae said, "I noted that 50% of $120 is $60."

5 "Mrs. Riley-Smith bought 30% of them for $129.78."

6 "My brother-in-law paid $34.50; he saved over 5%."

7 Shawn did all the work--Joanna got all the credit.

8 "Mrs. Alan-Tomly--and her daughter--were present."

27D Check Progress

1. Set the line spacing to DS, and set a 0.5" tab. Key the paragraph at a slow, controlled pace.

2. Key one or more 1' timed writings on the paragraph. Determine your rate. Try to increase your speed on each timing.

             •   4   •   8
     You may need to look at the keyboard now and
        •   12   •   16   •
then when you key numerals and symbols. Make the
   20   •   24   •   28
effort to learn each key location so that you can
        •   32   •   36   •
"keep your eyes on the copy." Try to make "eyes
   40   •   44   •   48
on the copy" your goal as you type numerals and
        •   52   •   56   •
symbols, such as %, -, and $, in your documents.

5C Practice Right Shift Key

Key the drill lines twice. SS lines and DS between 2-line groups.

Technique Guide

To key the capital letters of keys controlled by your left hand, use the right shift key.

1. Locate the **Right Shift** key on your keyboard.
2. Place your fingers on the home keys. Reach with your right fourth (little) finger to the **Right Shift** key.
3. Press the **Right Shift** key all the way down while you strike a letter key with a finger on your left hand.
4. Release the **Right Shift** key and quickly bring your finger back to home position.

Right Shift reach

```
1   F; F; F Ask Sam or Frank.  Fill the mill. Dan Ross
2   Eggs Road Sell Fans All X Tog Thad Earl Dan Exhale

3   Dan ran a light.  Sam Rose is here.  An X is here.
4   Al is fair game.  Ellen has a hat. Sara left home.

5   Alamo Dari Shelia Fred Frank Ron Rose Earl Xiao Do
6   Ask Dan for a hat.  Fran and Sam; Jan and Dean; If
```

5D Check Progress

Key the drill lines twice. SS lines and DS between 2-line groups.

Spacing Guide

■ Do not space between a . (period) and the word it follows.

■ Space twice after a . (period) at the end of a sentence when it is followed by another sentence.

```
1   n nj an; r rf for ; . .1 .1; an and; or for; nj rf
2   His name is Dan Lee.  Ask Jim or Sam or Al for it.

3   Nan or I shall fix the fig jam and send it to Kim.
4   Rose sent a taxi.  Kim and Jan set a log jam free.

5   Kiln Kill Jon Holm Lodge Noll Milk Ill Oman Island
6   Alfred Shelia Deila Freeda Earl Ron Tom Gail Xiaon
```

Lesson 27
- , " , and % Keys

Objectives

1. To improve control of - (hyphen), " (quotation), and % (percent) keys.
2. To improve control of **Space Bar**, **Tab**, and **Return/Enter** keys.

27A Review

Key the drill lines twice. SS lines and DS between 2-line groups.

All Letters 1 Jack C. Wesse explored the big, foggy quartz mine.

All Numbers 2 Order 48 cokes, 129 pies, 75 cakes, and 360 malts.

Shift Key 3 Sue James, Al Kent, and Jan Bowen met in New York.

Speed 4 Sign the pay form and they may do the work for me.

27B Focus on - , ", and % Keys

1. Locate the - (hyphen), " (quotation) and % (percent) keys on the keyboard chart at the right. Practice the reach to each key.

2. Key the lines twice; SS with a DS between 2-line groups.

Practice Guide

Reach to each new key with the correct finger:

    - (hyphen)—right fourth finger

    " (quotation)—right fourth finger

    % (percent)—left first finger and **Right Shift**

1 ;-; ;-; ;-; tune-up tune-up send-off send-off ;-;-
2 ;"; ;"; ;"; "It won't work." "I can see." "Do it."
3 f%f f%f 5f%f 50% 40% 89% f%f 149% The rate is 12%.
4 ;-; ;-; ;"; ;"; f%f f%f know-how right-of-way 8-12
5 ;-; say-so nitty-gritty free-for-all walkie-talkie
6 "I own 50% of the store." "I can go." "Mary is."

Lesson 6
V, U, and Q Keys

Objectives

1. To improve control of **v**, **u**, and **q** keys.
2. To improve control of **Space Bar** and **Return/Enter** keys.

6A Review

Key the drill lines twice. SS lines and DS between 2-line groups.

Practice Guide

Keep your hands and arms quiet.

```
1   n nj an; r rf for; . .l .l; an and; or for; nj rf;
2   I might not go; Sam has a sax.   Neal has six oars.

3   Jim asked if he had to find names for six lagoons.
4   Kim and Jan ate lots of tarts.   Go home Rex; I do.
```

6B Focus on V, U, and Q Keys

1. Locate the **v**, **u**, and **q** keys on the keyboard chart at the right. Practice the reach to each key.
2. Key the lines twice; SS with a DS between 2-line groups.

Practice Guide

Reach to each new key with the correct finger:

  v—left first finger

  u—right first finger

  q—left fourth finger

```
1   v v vf vf via via; u u uj uj us us; q q qa qa aqua
2   v vf via; u uj us; q qa aqua; Val likes to fix it.

3   us use use just just; aqua aqua quit quit; via via
4   fvf juj aqa; via via via; us us us; aqua aqua aqua

5   Val ate five figs.   Jan is quiet.   I shall mix it.
6   James asked if he had to move the six rugs for us.
```

26C Focus on $ and ' Keys

1. Locate the $ (dollar) and ' (apostrophe) keys on the keyboard chart at the right. Practice the reach to each key.

2. Key the lines twice; SS with a DS between 2-line groups.

Practice Guide

Reach to each new key with the correct finger:

$ (dollar)—left first finger and **Right Shift**

' (apostrophe)—right fourth finger

Spacing Guide

- Do not space between $ (dollar) and the number that follows it.

- Do not space before or after ' (apostrophe) within a word.

1 fr4f $f $4 f$f f$ $4 $81 f $90 $39 $f4 $29 $92 $

2 ;' ;'; ;'; ;'; I'll we've you'll don't can't Joe's

3 fr4f $4 $4; ';' ;'; $59 Jay's bicycle cost $48.18.

4 I'm, we'll, can't, and don't are all contractions.

5 Tom's, Bob's, Joanna's, and Jan's cats have fleas.

6 The items cost $29, $38, $129, $293, $90, and $49.

7 Bill's sister and Rile's brother play in the band.

8 Maria's house sold for $104,000 after thirty days.

26D Check Progress

1. Set the line spacing to DS, and set a 0.5" tab. Key the paragraph at a slow controlled pace.

2. Key one or more 1' timed writings on the paragraph. Determine your rate. Try to increase your speed on each timing.

```
            •        4        •        8
     Today I may earn as much as $4.  I have
  •              12          •          16
$48.13 in the bank.  Jay doesn't have this much
  •         20          •         24          •
money because he bought a new bicycle.  This is
  28          •         32          •         36
Jay's new bicycle.  He paid $85.14 for it at
      •         40
Helen's Cycle Shop.
```

6C Build Skill

Key the drill lines twice. SS lines and DS between 2-line groups.

Practice Guide

Lines 6, 7, and 8 contain all letter keys practiced thus far. Use them for extra practice.

1   n nj nj and; r rf rf fir; Ask Don M. Frank for it.
2   an and hand; or for form; Jan Roan; Susan E. Alan;

3   Joaquin asked if he had to move six rugs for them.
4   Tom Hale got it. Henri IX Lake lost all the mail.

5   Quin sang five songs for us and then quit singing.
6   Val Quin likes the task of fixing old marine jugs.

7   Jake might fix a sextant and give it to Luis Quar.
8   Jamie and Quin asked for the five or six old jugs.

6D Practice Return/Enter

Key the drill lines once. Strike the **Return/Enter** key after each group of words. (Groups of words are separated by vertical lines. Do not key the vertical lines.)

Practice Guide

Keep the other fingers of your right hand over the home keys as you strike the **Return/Enter** key with your right fourth finger.

1   an and hand|or for form|Janna Roane|Susan E. Alan|
2   via vial|van five;|us dusk|due rut;|qua aqua aqua|

3   six fix hex;|quad quid quit|aqua six fix|vet veal|
4   gnu glue;|guilt gulf guise;|gum gust gurgle|guard|

5   vial vile veil|queen quit|quiet quote|vest van VA|
6   veneer velvet|quilt quite|vender Venetian|vet gun|

7   Velia has quit.|Van quoted Gus.|Remain quiet.|No.|
8   Five jugs are here.|Luisa and Quin fixed the van.|

Lesson 26
$ and ' Keys

Objectives

1. To improve control of **$** (dollar) and **'** (apostrophe) keys.
2. To improve control of **Space Bar**, **Tab**, and **Return**/**Enter** keys.

26A Review

Key the drill lines twice. SS lines and DS between 2-line groups.

All Letters   1   A large fawn jumped quickly over white zinc boxes.

All Numbers   2   Pack 123 books, 48 pencils, 95 pads, and 670 pens.

Space Bar   3   Jim may pay many men to fix the map room for them.

Speed   4   He may do the work for us and then go to the city.

26B Improve Techniques:
Word Response

Key the drill lines twice. SS lines and DS between 2-line groups.

1 of or us me am by due pay them form such with paid

2 go with me; go with me to the; go with me to their

3 did can may us he she all not do see you the up of

4 She may go with me to the city to visit with them.

Lesson 7
Y, C, and P Keys

Objectives

1. To improve control of **y**, **c**, and **p** keys.
2. To improve control of **Space Bar** and **Return/Enter** keys.

7A Review

Key the drill lines twice. SS lines and DS between 2-line groups.

Practice Guide

Strike each key with a quick-snap stroke.

1 v vf via; u uj us; q qa aqua; Val likes to fix it.
2 Val ate five figs. Jan is quiet. I shall mix it.

3 James asked if he had to move the six rugs for us.
4 Van and Joe said all the questions are quite hard.

7B Focus on Y, C, and P Keys

1. Locate the **y**, **c**, and **p** keys on the keyboard chart at the right. Practice the reach to each key.
2. Key the lines twice; SS with a DS between 2-line groups.

Practice Guide

Reach to each new key with the correct finger:

   y—right first finger

   c—left second finger

   p—right fourth finger

1 y yj yj jay jay; c cd cd cod cod; p p; p; pal pal;
2 p; jay cod pal; Jay is my pal. The cod is a fish.

3 y yj jay; c cd cod; p p; pal; jay cod pal yj cd p;
4 yes yell young; can call cold; poke pan; peel copy

5 Jay and his pal caught a cod. They ate six perch.
6 Jay Vegam quickly typed a story in the fixed code.

25C Build Speed and Accuracy

1. Set the line spacing to DS, and set a 0.5" tab.

2. Key a 1' timed writing on each paragraph. Circle your errors.

3. Determine your rate. The number at the end of each line shows how many words you have keyed when you finish the line. Use the numbers at the bottom of the page to count the words keyed in an unfinished line. Add the two numbers to find the total words you keyed. Use the 1' scale for 1' writings and the 3' scale for 3' writings.

4. Key one or more 3' timed writings on the paragraphs. Try to key at the same rate (or faster) as you did on the 1' writings.

	1'	3'
There was once a lovely mountain nymph named Echo, who	11	4
loved to talk. She talked all day long and always had the	22	7
last word on any subject.	28	9
One day Echo and the other nymphs were with Zeus, the	10	13
highest of the Greek gods. Suddenly Hera, the wife of Zeus,	23	17
appeared. Echo quickly began to talk to Hera while the	34	21
other nymphs hurried away. When Hera realized how Echo had	46	25
tricked her, she decided to punish her. The punishment was	58	29
that Echo would never be able to start a conversation again.	70	33
She would only be able to reply. Echo would have the last	82	37
word, but that was all she would have.	90	39
This punishment was cruel indeed. Echo fell in love	10	43
with a young hunter but was unable to win his love with her	22	47
kind words. Echo was so disappointed that she went to hide	34	51
in the mountains and cliffs. Her love for this hunter	45	54
completely exhausted her, and her body gradually faded away.	58	59
The only thing that remained was her voice, which still	69	62
answers if you call.	73	64

1' | 1 | 2 | 3 | 4 | 5 | 6 | 7 | 8 | 9 | 10 | 11 | 12 |
3' | 1 | 2 | 3 | 4 |

7C Build Skill

Key the drill lines twice. SS lines and DS between 2-line groups.

Practice Guide

Strike the **Space Bar** with a quick down-and-in motion of the thumb. Release the **Space Bar** quickly.

```
1   yam yam couple couple party party yard yards yarns
2   copy copy Polly Polly yes yes yacht yacht yak yaks

3   years yearn yearly poorly canopy yeast Yeats yelps
4   yet Yemen yield pocket place pick pecan peck youth

5   Percy ate the yogurt.   The farmer picked the corn.
6   Place the yule log in the fire.   Copy the letters.
```

7D Find Errors

1. Study the illustration, which shows some common keying errors. Each error is circled and identified below the illustration.

2. Key the drill lines below the illustration and print. Find and circle each word in which you made an error.

Rule

Do not count more than one error in a word. Even if you make two mistakes in the same word, count only one error.

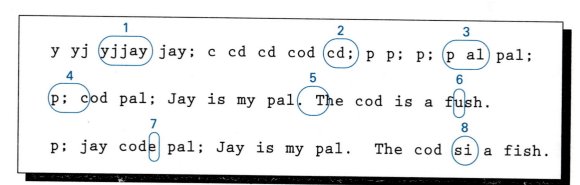

1 failure to space	5 incorrect spacing
2 omitted letter	6 wrong letter
3 extra space	7 extra letter
4 omitted word	8 transposed letters

```
1   Jay and his pal caught a cod.   They ate six perch.
2   Jay Vegam quickly typed a story in the fixed code.

3   Valerie had good training in manners in her youth.
4   You may run and jump on the dirt playground track.
```

Lesson 25
Build Skill

Objectives

1. To increase keying speed and accuracy.
2. To improve keying techniques.

25A Review

Key the drill lines twice. SS lines and DS between 2-line groups.

Practice Guide

- Keep your wrists low, but not resting on the desk or keyboard.
- Keep your fingers deeply curved.

One-Hand Words
1 you were, my opinion, are you, tax upon, after him
2 In my opinion, you should read only the tax cases.

Balanced-Hand Words
3 and the and then, and their, work for the, do it,
4 He did do the work for them by the end of the day.

All Letters
5 Jack Mead won first prize by solving the tax quiz.
6 Quincy Pamkez gave six bushels of wheat to Jarard.

25B Review Number Keys

Key the drill lines twice. SS lines and DS between 2-line groups.

Practice Guide

Keep your fingers curved and upright when reaching to the top row.

1 and 2 1 11 12 21 22 21 Do you have 11 students in Room 22?
3 and 4 2 33 44 34 43 33 Are there 33 or 44 toys in the box?
5 and 6 3 55 66 56 65 There are 5 men over age 66 attending.
7 and 8 4 77 88 78 87 78 The score was 77 to 88 at halftime.
9 and 0 5 00 99 90 09 90 Of the 90 women, only 9 were ready.

6 Total 1 and 20 and 83 and 49 and 57 and 16 and 20.
7 Reserve rooms 102, 653, and 1978 for September 24.

All Numbers
8 Buy 1,785 birds, 20 bison, 34 lions, and 69 seals.
9 What is the sum of 150 and 273 and 849 and 13,295?
10 Ship 32 files, 156 pens, 48 desks, and 790 chairs.

Lesson 8
W, B, and , Keys

Objectives

1. To improve control of **w**, **b**, and , (comma) keys.
2. To improve control of **Space Bar** and **Return/Enter** keys.

8A Review

Key the drill lines twice. SS lines and DS between 2-line groups.

Practice Guide

Try to increase your speed as you key each line the second time.

1 aqua via voice quit Luis copy cold youth yell pick
2 jumpy calm vest quiet kick six Percy quest yes yea

3 P. McCoy sits calmly to quiet his fear of heights.
4 Mary can quickly copy the recipes for yeast rolls.

8B Focus on W, B, and , Keys

1. Locate the **w**, **b**, and , (comma) keys on the keyboard chart at the right. Practice the reach to each key.
2. Key the lines twice; SS with a DS between 2-line groups.

Practice Guide

Reach to each new key with the correct finger:

    w—left third finger

    b—left first finger

    , (comma)—right second finger

1 w ws ws sow sow; b bf bf fob fob , ,k ,k sow, sow,
2 sew, saw, was, bat, bill, been, west, well, bought

3 bow, bed, boast, bath, button, beef, beauty, bench
4 write, willow, wand, wind, walk, wind, woman, wood

5 Bobby and his playmate, Wylie, will go with Carol.
6 Bobby and Wally, I think, will work well with you.

24C Check Progress

1. Set the line spacing to DS, and set a 0.5" tab.
2. Key a 1' timed writing on each paragraph. Circle your errors.
3. Determine your rate. The number at the end of each line shows how many words you have keyed when you finish the line. Use the numbers at the bottom of the page to count the words keyed in an unfinished line. Add the two numbers to find the total words you keyed. Use the 1' scale for 1' writings and the 3' scale for 3' writings.
4. Key one or more 3' timed writings on the paragraphs. Try to key at the same rate (or faster) as you did on the 1' writings.

	1'	3'
This is the story of two country sparrows who came to	10	3
the big city to live. They thought they might like the	22	7
bright lights of the big city. With this in mind, they	33	11
built their new home in a spot that had much hustle and	44	15
bustle right outside their door. Their new home even had a	56	19
special green light that went on and off. The two country	68	23
sparrows had selected a traffic signal for their new home.	80	27
But now the story takes on a sad aspect. The sparrows	11	31
were just about ready to move into their new home when a man	23	35
came along in a city truck. The excited birds could only	34	38
watch as he quickly yanked their nest out of the green	45	42
signal light.	48	43
I guess the sparrows did not realize that the special	10	47
spot they had selected for their new home was not zoned for	22	51
sparrow nests, or else they had neglected to get a building	34	55
permit. Whatever the reason, this is the end of the story	46	59
about the two country birds who tried living in a big city.	58	63
They decided that country living was best after all.	69	66

```
1' |  1  |  2  |  3  |  4  |  5  |  6  |  7  |  8  |  9  |  10  |  11  |  12  |
3' |       1       |       2       |       3       |       4       |
```

8C Build Skill

Key the drill lines twice. SS lines and DS between 2-line groups.

Practice Guide

Line 8 contains all letter keys practiced thus far. Use it for extra practice.

1 jay jay jay cod cod cod pal pal pal bow bow bow by
2 woodwork, rainbow, shoe box, worm, world, wide row

3 basket, bobbin, borrow, blossom, blue, bone, break
4 back body bowel, cab boy buy, bomb few, frown bowl

5 A taxi cab stopped at the curb, and a man got out.
6 Ten red balloons were released in the town square.

7 Mel Q. Jaffy was excused to begin the paving work.
8 John Pewters quickly calmed five or six big bears.

8D Improve Accuracy

1. Key the drill lines once at a slow steady pace.
2. Find and circle each word in which you made an error.
3. Count your errors. If you count more than two errors in a line, key the line again.

1 for five got big hay hand jug may kid loam old pay
2 Jan will move quickly to fix the big roped arenas.

3 J. Fork moved to a new place by the existing quay.
4 Rex Robeji quickly was named governor of Fatehpur.

5 Apple, oranges, and grapes are in the fruit salad.
6 Shelia and her father followed her coach in a car.

7 Alberta saw the frog flop quickly on the lily pad.
8 Velma turned on her computer, printer, and camera.

Lesson 24
Build Skill

Objectives

1. To increase keying speed and accuracy.
2. To improve keying techniques.

24A Review

Key the drill lines twice. SS lines and DS between 2-line groups.

Practice Guide

Strike **Return/Enter** quickly at line endings without spacing.

y
1 y yj jay yam hay; by any you; may day tray; buy yj
2 Yes, you may buy yams or hay any day of this week.

z
3 z za azure zone; zero zinc quiz; zest quizzical za
4 Zeres became dizzy during the quiz on zoning laws.

All Letters
5 Jack Dahlm saw five or six pigs by the quaint zoo.
6 Jeff Page quickly moved a zinc box to a warehouse.

24B Improve Techniques

Key the drill lines twice. SS lines and DS between 2-line groups.

Practice Guide

- Keep your eyes on the book.
- Key at an even pace without pauses.

One-Hand Words
1 on we up as in are you was him dear only were upon
2 were you; only tax; only a few; upon him; area oil
3 Was he aware that only a few areas could be taxed?

Balanced-Hand Words
4 he am to do so and the for may with them make work
5 if it is; to do so; and the; with them; their work
6 He or the men may go with me and pay for the work.

Long Reaches
7 Ed Cecil brought a number of bright union jackets.
8 That symphony played many unusual musical numbers.
9 Many players throw a minimum of brisk curve balls.

Lesson 9
Z and ? Keys

Objectives

1. To improve control of **z** and **?** (question mark) keys.
2. To improve control of **Space Bar** and **Return/Enter** keys.

9A Review

Key the drill lines twice. SS lines and DS between 2-line groups.

Practice Guide

Keep fingers curved as you reach to the first and third rows.

1   w ws sow; , ,k sow, b bf fob; sow fob wow big bow,
2   Bobby and Wally, I think, will work well with you.

3   Ben bowled a great game on Monday at Brower Lanes.
4   Mel Q. Jaffy was excused to begin the paving work.

9B Focus on Z and ? Keys

1. Locate the **z** and **?** (question mark) keys on the keyboard chart at the right. Practice the reach to each key.
2. Key the lines twice; SS with a DS between 2-line groups.

Practice Guide

Reach to each new key with the correct finger:

> **z**—left fourth finger
>
> **?** (question mark)—right fourth finger and **Left Shift**

1   z az za za za zoa zoa zoa zone zone zest zest zeal
2   a za zaz aza zoo zoo zoom zoom zeal zeal zest zest

3   ;? ;? ?; ? How? When? Where? Do you? May I go?
4   Did you bring any pens and pencils with you today?

5   Zela has a zeal and zest for life that is amazing.
6   Did a car zoom by? Is lemon zest used in the pie?

23C Build Skill

Key the drill lines twice. SS lines and DS between 2-line groups.

Practice Guide

Keep your fingers curved when reaching to the first or third row.

Third Row
1 You were to quote your best price on a typewriter.
2 Your quips are quite popular with your peer group.
3 You were to try to quote from the typewriter quiz.

First Row
4 Five or six men can mix the zinc in a box for Nan.
5 A number of men can fix the lynx cage in that zoo.
6 Robert struck a rich bonanza when mining the zinc.

Double Letters
7 The ragged puppy looked quizzically at the kitten.
8 Bill will appear at the drill meet in Mississippi.
9 Allen accepted a blue ribbon at the school bazaar.

23D Check Progress

1. Set the line spacing to DS, and set a 0.5" tab. Key a 1' timed writing on the Average paragraph at the right. Determine your rate.

2. Key one or more 1' timed writings on the Difficult paragraph. Try to key at the same rate as you did on the Average paragraph.

Average

        •   4   •   8
    They may send the card to that address. It
    •   12   •   16   •
was requested that they do this and that the case
20   •   24   •   28
be referred to the judge for action. The judge
        •   32   •   36   •
may be able to give us his decision by the end of
        40
the day.

Difficult

        •   4   •   8
    It is no exaggeration to say that a decrease
    •   12   •   16
in rainfall has resulted in water reserves that
20   •   24   •   28
are far below the average required for safety.
        •   32   •   36   •
New plans may be made to make a study of the water
        40
problem.

9C Build Skill

Key the drill lines twice. SS lines and DS between 2-line groups.

Spacing Guide

Space twice after a **?** (question mark) at the end of a sentence when it is followed by another sentence.

1 z z z za za zip zinc zone azure zeal zest zoom fez
2 ;?; ;?; ?;?? Now? When? Up? Down? What? When?

3 What is your ZIP code? Which zone is shown there?
4 Should I mail the work to Zela Zion in Zula, Ohio?

5 Did Mary Fox send the letters by General Delivery?
6 Can Maria spell zips, zinc, haze, quiz, and quart?

7 Is he going? Did you take the quiz? Is it right?
8 Hamp Cox will get five dozen quarts of bakery jam.

9D Practice Return/Enter

Key the drill lines once. Strike the **Return/Enter** key after each group of words. (Groups of words are separated by vertical lines. Do not key the vertical lines.)

Practice Guide

Keep the other fingers of your right hand over the home keys as you strike the **Return/Enter** key with your right fourth finger.

1 see Zula Zambia|scroll on down|write in the boxes|
2 zest zoom zeal|zone zoo zero|zip zinc Zion zombie|

3 a dish with zing|no zinc oxide|Zurich Switzerland|
4 Did he study zoology?|Was Mr. Ryan the zookeeper?|

5 May I see your copy?|Where are the zoo brochures?|
6 roll around|send to Mrs. West|find a right answer|

7 mop Jill Polly|nip you;|in on up hi|hill kiln mom|
8 fast tear saw|tax gate vest|zest sex dad|car Zeda|

Lesson 23
Build Skill

Objectives
1. To increase keying speed and accuracy.
2. To improve keying techniques.

23A Review

Key the drill lines twice. SS lines and DS between 2-line groups.

Practice Guide

Key slowly the first time you key a line to master the motions. As you key a line a second time, try to make each motion a bit faster.

v
1 v vf vow five; over pave gave; very rivet brave vf
2 Verner vowed to save five brave savages from harm.

w
3 w ws wow sow; tow was swell; with winter powwow ws
4 Wild winter winds will whip waves over that wharf.

x
5 x xs six fix; wax next relax; tax lax vex; extra x
6 The extra taxes due next week vexed the six women.

All Letters
7 Harv closed few mine exits by jagged quartz peaks.
8 Jak Prim saw a covey of quail and the big zoo fox.

23B Improve Techniques

1. Use the default tabs for your word processor or set tabs at 1' intervals.
2. Key the lines twice; SS with a DS between 2-line groups. Strike the **Tab** key where a → (right arrow) appears in lines 1 and 2.

Tab
1 aim → bat → car → date → even
2 fast → gale → have → item → jail

Space Bar
3 and the and the and the and the and the and the an
4 Jim or the men may pay them now for the many maps.

Shift Keys
5 F; F; Ja Ja; Fran McNut; Al Paul; Jan Tomas; Ja F;
6 Jan Tomas, A. Paul, and F. McNut met in St. Louis.

Lesson 10
:, Tab, and Backspace Keys

Objectives

1. To improve control of : (colon), **Tab**, and **Backspace** keys.
2. To improve control of **Space Bar** and **Return/Enter** keys.

10A Review

Key the drill lines twice. SS lines and DS between 2-line groups.

Practice Guide

Keep your eyes on the book as you key.

```
1   aid big cod did end for got ham if jam key lap man
2   nap of pal quay rod sue the us vow wig six yam zoo

3   Scroll down to see a chart, a letter, and numbers.
4   Will Jim Bogg check parts five and six of my quiz?
```

10B Focus on : and Tab Keys

1. Locate the : (colon) and **Tab** keys on the keyboard chart at the right. Practice the reach to each key.

2. Use the default tabs for your word processor or set tabs at 1' intervals.

3. Key the lines twice; SS with a DS between 2-line groups. Strike the **Tab** key where a → (right arrow) appears.

Practice Guide

Reach to each new key with the correct finger:

   : (colon)—right fourth finger and **Left Shift**

   Tab—left fourth finger

```
1   : ; : ; :: To:  From:  Date:  Time:  :;: :: :;: ::
2   Order these items:  marker, paper, tape, and glue.

3   The team consists of:  Jerima, Thomas, and Connie.
4   The box contains:  chicken, fish, fries, and salt.

5   wrong  →  right  →  before  →  after  →  overall
6   March  →  April  →  May    →  June  →  October
```

22C Force Speed

In each group of three lines at the right, the sentences progress in difficulty. The first sentence is easy. The second sentence is average. The third sentence is difficult.

1. For each group, key two 1' timed writings on each line in the group. Use the scale under the lines to determine your rate. Compare your rates on the six writings.

2. Key additional 1' writings on the sentence in each group on which you had the lowest rate.

Easy 1 Also, she may make their six men pay for the form.
Average 2 The chairman of the union may testify for the man.
Difficult 3 You were to get my opinion only on the estate tax.

1' | 1 | 2 | 3 | 4 | 5 | 6 | 7 | 8 | 9 | 10 |

Easy 4 She may go with them to do the work for the widow.
Average 5 Did she send a statement to the firm on that date?
Difficult 6 Was he to quote a minimum rate on the reserve oil?

1' | 1 | 2 | 3 | 4 | 5 | 6 | 7 | 8 | 9 | 10 |

Easy 7 It is right to make them sign for the right forms.
Average 8 Ask that man to visit our service department soon.
Difficult 9 In my opinion, the average minimum reserve is low.

1' | 1 | 2 | 3 | 4 | 5 | 6 | 7 | 8 | 9 | 10 |

22D Check Progress

1. Set the line spacing to DS, and set a 0.5" tab. Key a 1' timed writing on the paragraph at a controlled pace. Determine your rate.

2. Add four words to your rate. This will be your new goal.

3. Key three 1' timed writings on the paragraph. Try to reach your goal rate on each writing.

```
                        •                4                •                8
     Aim for a high goal and then work in the
         •                12                •                16
right way to reach that goal.  All your keying
     •                20                •                24                •
tasks will be quite easy if you plan your work and
28                •                32                •                36
then work your plan.  Be sure to do your very
         •                40                •                44                •
best; there will be no prize at all for work that
     48                •
is second best.
```

10C Build Skill

Key the drill lines once. SS lines and DS between 2-line groups. Strike the **Tab** key where a → (right arrow) appears.

Spacing Guide

- Do not space between a : (colon) and the word it follows.
- Space twice after a : (colon) used as punctuation (except in times).

1	Key this drill: z z zz za za zip zinc zone azure.							
2	Route the memo to: Hamad, Karen, Wilbur, and Joe.							
3	zest	→	zing	→	Zelia	→	zeal	→	zoomed
4	copy	→	delete	→	paste	→	insert	→	linked
5	Reds	→	Bears	→	Lions	→	Colts	→	Saints
6	Utah	→	Maine	→	Ohio	→	Idaho	→	Texas
7	To:	→	From:	→	Date:	→	Copy:	→	Time:
8	When:	→	What:	→	Why:	→	Who:	→	Where:

10D Practice Backspace Key

Key the drill lines once. In lines 1–6, strike the **Backspace** key where a ← (left arrow) appears. In lines 7 and 8, strike **Backspace** to delete any keying errors you make as you key.

Technique Guide

The **Backspace** key is used to delete text to the left of the cursor.

- Strike the **Backspace** key with your right fourth finger.
- Keep the other fingers of your right hand over the home keys as you strike the **Backspace** key.

1. recorded←←ing informing←←←ation roadwwu←←ay
2. Read the letter←←←←←←report to me, please.
3. Zelda Johnson←← wrotes← the newslettr←er.
4. Order fivw←e dox←zen boz←xes of stationery.
5. Start eacl←h new linne←←e without a pause.
6. Spacee← quickle←y and keeping←←← the thumb curved.
7. Paul saw six zebras as he and his pals ate apples.
8. My only regret is that I did not get your opinion.

Lesson 22
Build Skill

Objectives
1. To increase keying speed and accuracy.
2. To improve keying techniques.

22A Review

Key the drill lines twice. SS lines and DS between 2-line groups.

Practice Guide

- Keep your eyes on the book.
- Key at a steady, even pace.
- Strike each key with a quick-snap stroke.

s
1 s so us is sue; soap ask pass; sow six sick assist
2 Sue is to assist us when we make six bars of soap.

t
3 t tf the fit; tug tub tot; but butt butter; pat tf
4 Tony tossed the battered ball into the butter tub.

u
5 u uj us fur; jug hum numb; due cue gum; pup rut uj
6 An unusual number of gum rubber jugs will be used.

All Letters
7 Five or six big jays quickly seized the new lamps.
8 Judd L. Bright was very quick to fix many zippers.

22B Improve Techniques

Key the drill lines twice. SS lines and DS between 2-line groups.

3rd & 4th Fingers
1 azo six aqua pal was load wax soap poll quip apple
2 six loops; a load of soap; wax apples; an aqua pal
3 Paul saw six wasps as he ate apples and lollipops.

Double-Letter Words
4 all look drill meet week will glass tell need keep
5 all will look; see a meet; will need a class drill
6 Betty will need a class drill for the weekly meet.

Lesson 11
Build Skill

Objectives

1. To increase keying speed and accuracy.
2. To improve keying techniques

11A Review

Key the drill lines twice. SS lines and DS between two-line groups.

```
1    aid big cod did end for got ham if jam key lap man
2    nap of pal quay rod sue the us vow wig six yam zoo

3    ate bat car dad egg far get has ill just king live
4    many pool quick rose trust veal wheel tax yes zoom
```

11B Improve Techniques:
Home Row

Key the drill lines twice. SS lines and DS between two-line groups.

Practice Guide

Speed up your **Space Bar** action. Use a quick down-and-in motion of the right thumb.

```
1    asdf jkl; a;sldkfj had ask lag flag sag; ask a lad
2    dash glad gag lad fad dad; ask a lad; half a glass

3    lass gas fall ask had half gals gall sad fads hall
4    Hal; hag; false; kill; keg; asks; kiss; saddle had
```

21B Improve Techniques

Key the drill lines twice. SS lines and DS between 2-line groups.

Practice Guide

- Keep your fingers curved.
- Keep your hands and arms quiet.

Home Row
1 asdf jkl; jag ask has flag lad; asdf jkl; a;sldkfj
2 Jahl has half a glass; all lads had flags; ask dad
3 J. J. Jahl has had half a glass; all lads had hash

Third Row
4 aqua popoy was load deed liked for jug tug hay jay
5 you were; we wrote it; try to; key it or quote it;
6 Try to time these contestants with your stopwatch.

First Row
7 zinc lamb six jam cod numb vim box zoo men van ban
8 box cod; a big lynx; five or six men can mix zinc;
9 Jan vowed to coax a big fox into a box in the zoo.

21C Check Progress

1. Set the line spacing to DS, and set a 0.5" tab. Key a 1' timed writing on the paragraph at a controlled pace. Determine your rate.
2. Add four words to your rate. This will be your new goal.
3. Key three 1' timed writings on the paragraph. Try to reach your goal rate on each writing.

```
                                •               4                •               8
        The way you work and the way you key have a
        •               12              •               16              •
lot to do with your keying progress.  Just as
        20              •               24              •               28
there is a right way of working, there is a right
        •               32              •               36              •
way of keying.  Work in the right way by organizing
        40              •               44              •               48
your work.  Work right by keying with good form.
```

11C Build Skill

Key the drill lines twice. SS lines and DS between two-line groups.

Practice Guide

- Try to increase your speed as you key each line the second time.
- Use quick-snap strokes.

Home Row 1 a; sl dk fj gh hj asdf jkl; a;sldkfj ask all lads;

itm 2 i ik ik if if t tf tf fit fit m mj mj jam jam jam;

eox 3 e ed ed he he o ol ol doe doe x xs xs six six six;

nr. 4 n nj nj an an r rf rf for for . .l .l Jeff did it.

uvq 5 u uj uj us us v vf vf via via q qa qa aqua aqua aq

ycp 6 y yj yj jay jay c cd cd cod cod p p; p; pal pal p;

w,b 7 w ws ws sow sow , ,k ,k sow, ,k b bf fob fob bf bf

z?: 8 z za za zoa ? ?; ?; ;:; ;:; :: Pa? Do this: Try.

All Letters 9 Jim Bogg will check parts five and six of my quiz.

All Letters 10 Hamp Cox will get five dozen quarts of bakery jam.

11D Check Progress

1. Key a 1' timed writing on each line.
2. Determine the number of words per minute you key on each line.

Rule

Every five keystrokes (including letters, symbols, numbers, and spaces) are counted as one word. Use the scale at the bottom of the lines to count the number of words you key.

1 They did the work for us and she paid them for it.

2 Jack G. Zemsky will put five fresh quail in a box.

3 The right way of working is to hit the right keys.

4 Try to type right and keep your eyes on this copy.

5 Day by day if you try your typing skill will grow.

1' | 1 | 2 | 3 | 4 | 5 | 6 | 7 | 8 | 9 | 10 |

Lesson 21
Build Skill

Objectives

1. To increase keying speed and accuracy.
2. To improve keying techniques.

21A Review

Key the drill lines twice. SS lines and DS between 2-line groups.

Position Guide

- Fingers curved and upright over home keys
- Wrists low, but not touching keyboard
- Forearms parallel to slant of keyboard
- Body erect, sitting back in chair
- Feet on floor for balance
- Eyes on copy

p
1 p p; pal lap; ape apple pepper; pan pop popular p;
2 A popular ape ate an apple under the pepper trees.

q
3 q qa quay; aqua quart quince; quit quiet quick qa;
4 A. Quentin quickly and quietly ate the quince jam.

r
5 r rf rug rut rob; or for ore; their train brave rf
6 Robin worked for an hour before the train arrived.

All Letters
7 Kame brought prize jewels for very excited queens.
8 Jackie Dighz will move from Quincy next September.

Lesson 12
Build Skill

Objectives

1. To increase keying speed and accuracy.
2. To improve keying techniques.

12A Review

Key the drill lines twice—first slowly, then faster. SS lines and DS between two-line groups.

```
1   asdf jkl; dash glad sag lad fad hag; half a glass;
2   aid big cod did end for got ham if jam key lap man
3   nap of pal quay rod sue the us vow wig six yam zoo
```

12B Improve Techniques: Third Row

Key the drill lines twice. SS lines and DS between two-line groups

```
1   u uj q qa i ik w ws o ol e ed p p; r rf y yj t tf;
2   quit prey wow it or you pep quote ire were quite y
3   try to key; upper row; your keyboard is; to quote;
```

12C Build Skill

Key the drill lines twice. SS lines and DS between two-line groups.

```
1   and if; and if they; and if they go with me to the
2   do it; do it for them; do the work for them and me
3   Keying is exciting after you learn to key quickly.
```

12D Check Progress

1. Key a 1' timed writing on each line.
2. Determine the number of words per minute you key on each line.

```
1   Work in the right way and it will be easy to type.
2   The right way of working is the right way to work.
3   Jack marveled at big waxy pods for the quaint zoo.
```

1' | 1 | 2 | 3 | 4 | 5 | 6 | 7 | 8 | 9 | 10 |

20C Focus on 9 and 1 Keys

1. Locate the **9** and **1** keys on the keyboard chart at the right. Practice the reach to each key.

2. Key the lines twice; SS with a DS between 2-line groups.

Practice Guide

Reach to each new key with the correct finger:

9—right third finger

1—left fourth finger

```
1   lo91 91 91 99 99 99 lo91 92 93 94 96 97 95 98 99 9

2   aqla aqla al al aqla la la 11 11 aqla 18 19 13 12


3   lo91 91 91; 1 11 1,111; 19 191 1911; 12 13 14 1919

4   lo91 91 91; aqla la la; 19 191 1911; 12 13 14 1919


5   Key 19 and 91 and 99 and 48 and 37 and 26 and 501.

6   Read line 19 on page 191.  Packet 9 has 19 pieces.


7   I added 12 and 73 and 84 and 59 and 260 and 1,385.

8   Key these numbers:  8, 23, 45, 16, 98, 23, and 34.
```

20D Check Progress

1. Set the line spacing to DS, and set a 0.5" tab. Key the paragraph at a slow, well-controlled pace.

2. Key one or more 1' timed writings on the paragraph. Record your rate. Try to increase your speed on each timing.

```
                  •        4         •        8
     Today I learned the 9 and 1 keys.  Now I can
  •            12          •          16         •
key 9 and 1 and 4 and 8 and 3 and 7 and 2 and 6
     20            •            24         •         28
and 50.  I try to key each number quickly using
         •        32
the correct technique.
```

Lesson 13
Build Skill

Objectives

1. To increase keying speed and accuracy.
2. To improve keying techniques.

13A Review

Key the drill lines twice—first slowly, then faster. SS lines and DS between two-line groups.

Practice Guide

Try to hold hands and arms quiet.

```
1   quit pray wow it or you pep quote ire were quite y
2   aid aqua azure; sow swoop six; did due dock; qa za
3   for fit fog fib five; go got gib; ha hay hand; jhj
4   jug jay jam; key kick; load old; pal lap pop; p p;
```

13B Improve Techniques:
First Row

Key the drill lines twice. SS lines and DS between two-line groups

```
1   m mj z za n nj x xs , ,k c cd . .l v vf , , , b bf
2   jam zone next six cob vim box zinc mix move back z
3   move back; five boxes; next zone; mix zinc; he can
```

13C Build Skill

Key the drill lines twice. SS lines and DS between two-line groups.

Practice Guide

Keep your fingers curved and upright.

```
1   six of the men; a box of zinc; vim and vigor; move
2   Six of the men may move five boxes of zinc for us.
3   The men came to help us fix a cave in the big zoo.
```

13D Check Progress

1. Key a 1' timed writing on each line.
2. Determine the number of words per minute you key on each line.

```
1   Try to jump well and learn to jump with good form.
2   Hold your hands and arms quiet as you strike keys.
3   Next, have the men paint the safety zone and curb.
```

1' | 1 | 2 | 3 | 4 | 5 | 6 | 7 | 8 | 9 | 10 |

Lesson 20
9 and 1 Keys

Objectives

1. To improve control of **9** and **1** keys.
2. To improve control of **Space Bar**, **Tab**, and **Return/Enter** keys.

20A Review

Key the drill lines twice. SS lines and DS between two-line groups.

Practice Guide

Key slowly the first time you key a line to master the motions. As you key a line a second time, try to make each motion a bit faster.

```
m   1 m mj may make; am jam ham yam; me man mend small m
    2 A man may eat that ham.   My mother makes good jam.

n   3 n nj nap pan fan; an and hand; run dinner banner n
    4 Jan and Ann had dinner.   My name is on the banner.

o   5 o ol old cold; of over often; to do so go; look ol
    6 Otto often looked for gold near the old gold mine.

All Letters  7 The gray fox jumped quietly over lazy brown ducks.
             8 Six squawking zoo birds just arrived from Pahcayl.
```

20B Improve Techniques:
Space Bar Control

Key the drill lines twice. SS lines and DS between two-line groups.

Practice Guide

Strike the **Space Bar** with a quick down-and-in motion of the thumb.

```
1 or or or; to to to; if if if; us us us; or or for;
2 for for for; he he he; the the the; an an an; and;

3 and and and; and the and the and the; and if they;
4 He is to do it for us.   He is to do it for us now.

5 Work with me.   Did he do it by the end of the day?
6 Joe and I can go to the show if she will drive us.
```

Lesson 14
Build Skill

Objectives

1. To increase keying speed and accuracy.
2. To improve keying techniques.

14A Review

Key the drill lines twice—first slowly, then faster. SS lines and DS between two-line groups.

1 jam zone next six cob vim box zinc mix move back z
2 an and man; us usual you; of for do; end deed vie;
3 if fit like; old kick just end again; poll quail z
4 Six blazing jets zip skyward from that quay cover.

14B Improve Techniques:
Continuity

Key the drill lines twice. SS lines and DS between two-line groups.

Practice Guide

Space quickly after each word.

1 if it is; to do so; and the; She may go with them.
2 get you eat ill was him saw pop art joy add pin ::
3 She said that I was ill from eating too much food.

14C Build Skill

Key the drill lines twice. SS lines and DS between two-line groups.

1 She may go with them.   She may go with them today.
2 Do the work for me.   Do the work in the right way.
3 Did he do the work?   Did he do this work for them?

14D Check Progress

1. Key a 1' timed writing on each line.
2. Determine the number of words per minute you key on each line.

1 Bob may make a map of the big city for you and me.
2 Writing is easier when you learn to key correctly.
3 Jeff Page quickly moved a long box to a warehouse.

1' | 1 | 2 | 3 | 4 | 5 | 6 | 7 | 8 | 9 | 10 |

19C Focus on 5 and 0 Keys

1. Locate the **5** and **0** keys on the keyboard chart at the right. Practice the reach to each key.

2. Key the lines twice; SS with a DS between 2-line groups.

Practice Guide

Reach to each new key with the correct finger:

5—left first finger

0—right fourth finger

1 fr5f 5f 5f 55 55 55 fr5f ;p0; 0; 0; 00 00 00 ;0; 0

2 fr5f ;p0; f5 ;0 5f 0; 50 05 ;0; f5f 50 05 frf ;0;0

3 fr5f 5f 5f; ;p0; 0; 0; 5 55 0 00 50; 05 505 50, 50

4 f4f f5f f4f f5f 48 58 ;0; 20 30 40 50 70 05 60 808

5 Key 502 and 48 and 37 and 26 and 5,036 and 50,204.

6 Team 5 will meet in Room 50 at 8 a.m. on April 25.

7 Bake the cake at 350 degrees for about 50 minutes.

8 Use these numbers: 205, 305, 40, 505, 20, and 50.

19D Check Progress

1. Set the line spacing to DS, and set a 0.5" tab. Key the paragraph at a slow, controlled pace.

2. Key one or more 1' timed writings on the paragraph. Record your rate. Try to increase your speed on each timing.

```
                 •             4            •            8
     Today I learned the 5 and 0 keys.  Now I can
  •                12            •              16            •
key 5 and 0 and 4 and 8 and 3 and 7 and 2 and 6,
  20                 •              24             •             28
or I can key 506 and 55 and 505.  I key well with
  •                32
my fingers curved.
```

Lesson 15
Build Skill

Objectives
1. To increase keying speed and accuracy.
2. To improve keying techniques.

15A Review

Key the drill lines twice—first slowly, then faster. SS lines and DS between two-line groups.

1 aid big cod did end for got ham if jam key lap man
2 nap of pal quay rod sue the us vow wig six yam zoo
3 Peg saw jackals and foxes over by the quartz mine.

15B Improve Techniques:

Keystroking

Key the drill lines twice. SS lines and DS between two-line groups.

1 quiz quay aqua zoo zany pal lap polls loop was saw
2 six axle loss next quick look apple buzz wax squaw
3 Paul saw six zebras as he and his pals ate apples.

Practice Guide

Keep your fingers curved and upright.

15C Build Skill

1. Set the line spacing to DS, and set a 0.5" tab. Key two 1' timed writings on the paragraph. Try to increase your speed on the second timing.

2. Use the numbers and dots above the lines to determine the number of words per minute you key. (The dots between the numbers show a two-word count.)

```
                     •           4           •           8
       When you key, be sure you key right.  Do not
      •           12          •           16          •
look at the keys.  Trust your fingers to hit the
      20          •           24          •           28
right keys.  Keep your eyes here on this copy.
```

15D Check Progress

1. Key a 1' timed writing on each line.

2. Determine the number of words per minute you key on each line.

1 Paul keyed six zany quiz questions about that zoo.
2 Polly quickly filled those sacks with ripe apples.
3 Are you striking every key with an even keystroke?

1' | 1 | 2 | 3 | 4 | 5 | 6 | 7 | 8 | 9 | 10 |

Lesson 19
5 and 0 Keys

Objectives

1. To improve control of **5** and **0** keys.
2. To improve control of **Space Bar**, **Tab**, and **Return/Enter** keys.

19A Review

Key the drill lines twice. SS lines and DS between two-line groups.

Practice Guide

Keep up your pace to the end of a line, strike **Return/Enter** quickly, and begin the new line without a pause.

j
1 j jam jay jug; jet jab jot just; jail jelly jungle
2 A jungle jaguar jabbed his paw into the jelly jug.

k
3 k key kale kick; ask mask sick; deck pack sketch k
4 Rick is sick. Jack packed the deck keg with kale.

l
5 l lay land lend; glad roll slide; pail sail nail l
6 Polly will be glad to fill those pails with nails.

All Letters
7 Jeff Zobem gave and quickly typed the tax answers.
8 Many big jackdaws quickly zipped over the fox pen.

19B Improve Techniques:
Shift Key Control

Key the drill lines twice. SS lines and DS between two-line groups.

Practice Guide

Make the shift key reach with the little finger while keeping other fingers over the home keys.

1 F; F; F; Ja Ja Ja; Jack, Ellen, Kay, Tom, Paul, F;
2 Jim, Bob, and I may visit Tom and Jeb in New York.

3 Sue McAdams and Ellen James live in Waverly, Iowa.
4 James Alan, Henry Day, and Julian Vern walked out.

5 April, May, June, and July can be the best months.
6 Maria Perez and Kim Yung live near Columbus, Ohio.

Lesson 16
4 and 8 Keys

Objectives

1. To improve control of **4** and **8** keys.

2. To improve control of **Space Bar**, **Tab**, and **Return/Enter** keys.

16A Review

Key the drill lines twice. SS lines and DS between two-line groups.

Position Guide

- Fingers curved and upright over home keys
- Wrists low, but not touching keyboard
- Forearms parallel to slant of keyboard
- Body erect, sitting back in chair
- Feet on floor for balance
- Eyes on copy

a
1 a an and aid; sad dad fad gag; had jam kale land a
2 Laura ate a banana.   A lad may draw a map of Java.

b
3 b bf big bit; boy fob bid fib; tub rub able baby b
4 A big baby boy bit the rubber tube.   Bob fixed it.

c
5 c cd cod cut; cue cob sock neck; rock accept cow c
6 A cow ate corn cut form a cob.   Jack caught a cod.

All Letters
7 Fred James quickly solved the exciting bow puzzle.
8 Hazel Jacques will buy six tax maps for Dave King.

18C Focus on 2 and 6 Keys

1. Locate the **2** and **6** keys on the keyboard chart at the right. Practice the reach to each key.

2. Key the lines twice; SS with a DS between 2-line groups.

Practice Guide

Reach to each new key with the correct finger:

2—left third finger

7—right first finger

1	sw2s 2s 2s 22 22 22 sw2s jy6j 6j 6j 66 66 666 jy6j
2	sw2s jy6j s2 6j 26 62 26 63 64 27 28 23 62 67 68 6
3	sw2s 2s 2s; jy6j 6j 6j; 2 22 6 66 26; 62 626 2,626
4	Key 26 and 72 and 384 and 47 and 3,438 and 26,247.
5	By 6:32 a.m., 226 of the 2,237 pupils had arrived.
6	These 262 girls and 226 boys keyed Parts 6 and 22.
7	Reserve rooms 26, 36, 44, and 64 for September 14.
8	Buy 23 books, 266 pens, 364 pencils, and 278 pads.

18D Check Progress

1. Set the line spacing to DS, and set a 0.5" tab. Key the paragraph at a slow, controlled pace.

2. Key one or more 1' timed writings on the paragraph. Record your rate. Try to increase your speed on each timing.

```
                 •              4            •              8
      Today I learned the 2 and 6 keys.  Now I can
        •            12              •              16           •
key 4 and 8 and 3 and 7 and 2 and 6, or I can key
    20                •              24            •             28
372 and 26,487.  I reach with my fingers to key all
    •              32
these numbers.
```

16B Improve Techniques: Keystroking

Key the drill lines twice. SS lines and DS between two-line groups.

```
1   and aqua azure; pole old lap; was wax six; if like
2   kick; due end cod; jug jam jay ham hand; form five
3   fit fig fib; got tug big; hay yam any; and the and
```

16C Focus on 4 and 8 Keys

1. Locate the **4** and **8** keys on the keyboard chart at the right. Practice the reach to each key.

2. Key the lines twice; SS with a DS between 2-line groups.

Practice Guide

Reach to each new key with the correct finger:

4—left first finger

8—right second finger

```
1   fr4f 4f 4f 44 44 44 fr4f ki8k 8k 8k 88 88 88 ki8k8
2   fr4f ki8k f4 8k 48 84 48 fr4f ki8k f4 k8 f4 k8 848
3   fr4f 4f 4f; ki8k 8k 8k; 4 44 8 88 48; 84 848 4,848
4   Key 4 and 8 and 4 and 84.  Is the number 48 or 84?
5   The 48 men had 8 games.  The box is 4 inches wide.
6   The accident happened 4 miles from the I84 bridge.
```

16D Check Progress

1. Set the line spacing to DS, and set a 0.5" tab. Key the paragraph at a slow controlled pace.

2. Key one or more 1' timed writings on the paragraph. Try to increase your speed on each new timing.

3. Use the numbers and dots above the lines to determine the number of words per minute you key.

```
           •              4         •              8
        Today I learned to type 4 and 8.  It is easy
     •              12          •              16
    to type 4 and 8 if I keep my fingers well curved.
    20              •              24          •         28
    I also try to make the reach to the 4 and 8 with
     •              32
    my hands quiet.
```

Lesson 18
2 and 6 Keys

Objectives

1. To improve control of **2** and **6** keys.
2. To improve control of **Space Bar**, **Tab**, and **Return/Enter** keys.

18A Review

Key the drill lines at the right. SS lines and DS between two-line groups.

Spacing Guide

- Do not space after an internal period in an abbreviation.
- Space once after each period following initials.

g
1 g gf go got gave; rug bug tug; age again lag jag g
2 Gregg gave Gigi a golf ball during that golf game.

h
3 h hj hay hand; the then they their; though laugh h
4 They thanked him for the ham he brought for lunch.

i
5 i ik if it is; fit did big bit; lie like kick pail
6 Use i.e. for that is. J. I. Imiria is his sister.
No space ↑   One space ↑ ↑

All Letters
7 Zeb Fodec may give the queen six sparkling jewels.
8 Polly K. Fazzio bought six jacquard weaving looms.

18B Improve Techniques:
Tab Key Control

1. Use the default tabs for your word processor or set tabs at 1' intervals.
2. Key the lines twice; SS with a DS between 2-line groups. Strike the **Tab** key where a → (right arrow) appears.

1 to	→ do	→ so	→ is	→ good
2 if	→ it	→ is	→ not	→ here
3 and	→ the	→ man	→ is	→ late
4 work	→ with	→ them	→ on	→ the
5 time	→ to	→ read	→ all	→ lines
6 name	→ age	→ sex	→ date	→ class

Lesson 17
3 and 7 Keys

Objectives

1. To improve control of **3** and **7** keys.
2. To improve control of **Space Bar**, **Tab**, and **Return/Enter** keys.

17A Review

Key the drill lines twice. SS lines and DS between two-line groups.

Practice Guide

- Keep your eyes on the book.
- Key at a steady, even pace.
- Strike each key with a quick-snap stroke.

d 1 d do did due; add dad lad had; end odd dock dude d
   2 Dick fixed the dock for his dad. Can the lad add?

e 3 e ed end ended; lend feel are due; echo deck doe e
   4 Lee does not feel well. Eddie cleaned their deck.

f 5 f for fit fog fib five; fix fear golf; cuff fad f
   6 Fred fried five fish for them after the golf game.

All Letters 7 Spell the words: quartz, covey, jumbo, fox, king.
             8 Wolfe maximized skill just by improved techniques.

17B Improve Techniques:
Space-Bar Control

Key the drill lines twice. SS lines and DS between two-line groups.

1 if it is, if it is; and the, and the; and if it is
2 and the, and then, and their; work for them; do it

3 Many men may help you. Do this work for us today.
4 Edy decided to leave just before the tent arrived.

5 He may make them pay for the land when they visit.
6 They may go with us to do the work for the widows.

17C Focus on 3 and 7 Keys

1. Locate the **3** and **7** keys on the keyboard chart at the right. Practice the reach to each key.
2. Key the lines twice; SS with a DS between 2-line groups.

Practice Guide

Reach to each new key with the correct finger:

3—left second finger

7—right first finger

1 de3d 3d 3d 33 33 33 de3d ju7j 7j 7j 77 j77 77 ju7j

2 de3d ju7j 3d 7j 37 73 37 737 373 74 74 47 38 83 87

3 de3d 3d 3d; ju7j 7j 7j; 3 33 7 77 37; 73 737 3,737

4 Key 3 and 7 and 37 and 73 and 48 and 837 and 1483.

5 The 3 boys have 37 books. Jan has 7 blue ribbons.

6 Total 47 and 83 and 37 and 7 and 73 and 84 and 43.

17D Check Progress

1. Set the line spacing to DS, and set a 0.5" tab. Key the paragraph at a slow, controlled pace.
2. Key one or more 1' timed writings on the paragraph. Record your rate. Try to increase your speed on each timing.

Practice Guide

- To improve keystroking, align fingers correctly.
- Strike the **Space Bar** quickly after each word without pausing.

```
                            •          4              •              8
       Today I learned the 3 and 7 keys.  Now I can
     •                 12              •            16              •
 key 4 and 8 and 3 and 7, or I can key 4,837 and 37
  20              •            24              •            28
 and 84 and 73.  I try to key all number keys with
  •
 quiet hands.
```

Repetitive Stress Injury

Repetitive stress injury (RSI) is a result of repeated movement of a part of the body. A familiar example is "tennis elbow." Of more concern to keyboard users is the form of RSI called **carpal tunnel syndrome** (CTS).

CTS is a disease that develops gradually. With CTS the wrists, hands, and forearms can become inflamed and painful. CTS symptoms include:

• Numbness in the hand
• Tingling or burning the hand, wrist, or elbow
• Pain in the forearm, elbow, or shoulder
• Difficulty gripping objects

CTS is often a concern for workers who use a computer keyboard or mouse. The risk of developing CTS is less for people who use proper furniture and equipment, keyboarding techniques, posture, and/or muscle-stretching exercises than for those who do not. Keyboard users can reduce the risk of developing RSI/CTS by taking these precautions:

1. Arrange the workstation correctly: Position the keyboard directly in front of the chair. Keep the front edge of the keyboard even with the edge of the desk. Place the keyboard at elbow height. Place the monitor about 18 to 24 inches from your eyes with the top edge of the display screen at eye level.

2. Use a proper chair and sit correctly. Use a seat that allows you to keep your feet flat on the floor while you are keying. Sit erect and as far back in the seat as possible.

3. Use correct arm and wrist positions and movement. Keep your arms near the side of your body in a relaxed position. Your arms should be parallel to the floor and level with the keyboard. Your wrists should be in a flat, neutral position.

4. Use proper keyboarding techniques. Keep your fingers curved and upright over the home keys. Keep wrists and forearms from touching or resting on any surface while keying. Strike each key lightly using the fingertip.

5. Take short rest breaks. A rest of one to two minutes every hour is appropriate.

6. Exercise and stretch your neck, shoulders, arms, wrists, and fingers before beginning to key each day and often during the workday.

Finger Gymnastics

Brief daily practice of finger gymnastics will strengthen your finger muscles and increase the ease with which you key. Begin each keying period with this conditioning exercise. Choose two or more drills for this practice.

DRILL 1. Hands open, fingers wide, muscles tense. Close the fingers into a tight fist, with thumb on top. Relax the fingers as you straighten them. Repeat 10 times.

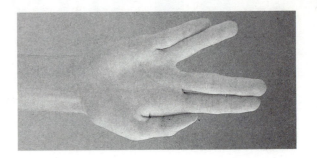

DRILL 2. Clench the fingers as shown. Hold the fingers in this position for a brief time; then extend the fingers, relaxing the muscles of fingers and hand. Repeat the movements slowly several times. Exercise both hands at the same time.

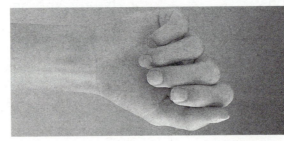

DRILL 3. Place the fingers and thumb of one hand between two fingers of the other hand, and spread the fingers as much as possible. Spread all fingers of both hands.

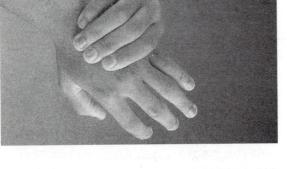

DRILL 4. Interlace the fingers of the two hands and wring the hands, rubbing the heel of the palms vigorously.

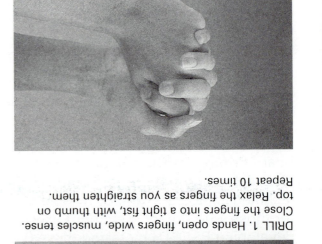

DRILL 5. Spread the fingers as much as possible, holding the position for a moment or two; then relax the fingers and lightly fold them into the palm of the hand. Repeat the movements slowly several times. Exercise both hands at the same time.

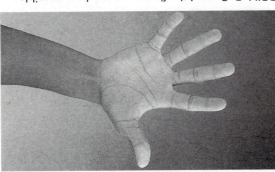

DRILL 6. Rub the hands vigorously. Let the thumb rub the palm of the hand. Rub the fingers, the back of the hand, and the wrist.

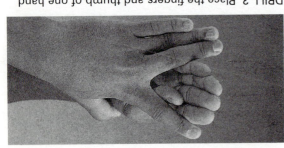

DRILL 7. Hold both hands in front of you, fingers together. Hold the last three fingers still and move the first finger as far to the side as possible. Return the first finger; then move the first and second fingers together; finally move the little finger as far to the side as possible.